NEW to B2B

A New Outside Sales Hunter's Guide to Finding and Selling New Accounts

by James Zimmerman

Acknowledgements

I would like to thank Maryann Cunningham for her encouragement and advisement. Without you, this book would not have been written. I would also like to thank my daughter Josephene Zimmerman for bearing me through my years of studying. Another person who influenced me is my good friend Chandler Benn who is a talented author whose mere existence inspired and continues to inspire me. Finally, James Brown who oddly enough taught me most of what I needed to know about working, selling and life in general. Without my Godfather there would be no book.

Table of Contents

Introduction

James Brown, the Godfather of Soul and friend of my family growing up once told me, "Jimmy, you can never stop hustlin'. You can never stop hustlin' because any day, any moment, everything you got can get taken away." He laughed as he went on, "And if and when it does get taken away - if you're a hustler; you can just go out there and get it again. You see this world that we're standing on moves because of hustlers. So, you just keep hustlin' boy. You'll get it."

This conversation happened when I was around eight or nine years old. I had been working on selling holiday cards from a catalog in order to earn a batch of sea monkeys. I signed up for the program from an add in the back of Boys Life magazine and it turned out the company was running a hustle and I had bought in hook line and sinker.

I sold a ton of holiday cards and when the little brown envelope came in the mail with the sea monkey eggs, I quickly tore it open and poured the dust into a fish bowl of water. Days and weeks went by but no sea monies ever appeared. Jipped!

What I did get was my first experience selling a product. More importantly was the advice I got from Mr. Brown that has lead me my entire life.

I wrote this book about selling B2B which is a type of selling that I find to be the most conducive for a life long student of the hustle. I have sold retail and houses - both of which I found to be very boring at times. Salespeople have to do a lot of waiting around for prospects to just come walking in.

Selling B2B is a job where the hustlers win. It doesn't matter how educated, smart, pretty, thin or how many other typical advantages you might have. All that matters is how long you can keep your feet moving to the beat. If you aren't having any luck you can always do something crazy to get luck to change your way.

That is why I love it. No boss with any brains will fire a hustler - even if he hates his guts. Hustlers bring in revenue and keep on bringing revenue and they don't need to be managed. Hustlers can hear the beat and they keep moving to it.

In this book I explain some of the very basics about sales process. You can get these basics in a lot of different books - but this book also will explain how to run your whole job the way a hustler will. Another bonus is that I don't pussyfoot around with a bunch of long stories about what a great salesperson I am. Hustlers don't need to brag - but I will tell you some of the secrets that I have developed on my own that make a huge difference.

In the chapters coming up you will learn about the basic sales process.

- Prospecting: In person and on the phone

- First meetings

- Presentations

- Taking the Sale

- Paperwork

- Follow up

Other sales books out there overcomplicate the sales process and spend a lot of time on qualifying. Personally, I believe that salespeople do not need to be told to qualify because they already find all kinds of ways to waste time and looking up a prospect's website or messing around on LinkedIn are great time wasters that would qualify as qualifying. While other AE's are qualifying hustlers are dialing that phone, walking in the back door of businesses and playing dumb about any information they do know about a prospect.

Some of the tips that I will recommend for any AE in this book are:

- Always keep score and I will explain how to do that so you stay moving regardless of what the slackers around you are doing.

- Sandbag your business to make yourself look like a consistent champ.

- Manipulate your quarterly numbers to make you look like a flippin rock star.

- How to overcome the dumbasses in your own company (I guarantee they are there)

At the end of the day, if you want to be successful in outside B2B selling, you have to live by one reality and that is: **It is all about bloody noses and bloody knuckles**.

If you are afraid of getting hit in the nose by a bunch of jerks who don't have time for you; you're going to have to get tougher. If you are afraid of telling a prospect that the best thing for their business in the world is to give you money for whatever you sell - then, you're going to have to get tougher. The only way to get over the fear of bloody noses and bloody knuckles that I know of is to pick up the phone and start dialing. The only way that I know to get over being a coward is to go walk into a business and ask to talk to the president of the company like he is in big shit if he doesn't talk to you.

In sales especially outside B2B sales we get calluses on our noses and knuckles and we just keep swinging because that is what hustlers have to do to survive.

You have to be willing to take the hits and get hit every day and keep on going - Rocky Balboa

Background

Some readers of this book might not be up to speed as to what B2B selling is. This next section is just a rudimentary explanation. If you are already familiar - just skim through until you get to the first chapter.

What is selling B2B?

Selling is the function of causing a transaction to happen through a combination of knowledge, ability, charisma and persuasion. This book will only deal with direct sales and will skip over the subjects of internet sales and customer service order taking. There are different types of direct selling:

Categories of Sales Jobs

Inside retail sales

Like furniture salespeople, car salespeople, cell phone salespeople. These jobs all more or less rely on a company's other marketing strategies to draw in prospects to sell to. There is some follow up involved but most inside sales people are expected to close their prospects in the first meeting. The ability to close these walk in prospects is a bit of an art form and the salespeople in these positions probably get more ongoing sales training than other sales jobs. The downside is that many of these jobs can see periods of time that are quite slow due to seasonality, weather conditions, poor economical conditions, increased credit scrutiny and a host of other conditions that are outside the control of the salesperson. During slow times, many average performing salespeople are laid off or permanently fired. Another problem during slow times is that companies often have too many salespeople on hand and so the environment can become like a pack of wolves snarling at each other over every prospect that walks through the door. Nobody wants to be fired so it does pay to be mean in these environments.

Outside retail sales

Insurance agents, real estate agents, construction salespeople and any salesperson that has to go out and hustle people are outside retail salespeople. These jobs also rely somewhat on a company's marketing but they can always make more calls so they do control their destinies a little more than the Inside Retail Salesperson. Many of these jobs are filled with people who are willing to work at night and weekends. This is because the people they need to sell to are at work during the weekdays. Because of their rather loose daytime schedules most chambers of commerce and other volunteer groups are loaded up with Outside Retail Salespeople where they do a lot of networking.

Inside Business to Business(B2B) Sales

Inside B2B selling is all about calling on or receiving calls from new business accounts and current customer reorders. A good

10

inside B2B salesperson will keep in contact with customers and be able to check on and manage any customer service concerns all the way through to delivery. These jobs sometimes involve face to face meetings and often these meetings can be had without travel using technologies like Go To Meeting, Google Hangouts or Skype. Ultimately, the secret to success in an inside B2B selling job is the ability to dial, speak clearly and connect over the phone with someone you may never see face to face. That takes a certain kind of person and there are several that make a very good living selling from an office. The work environment can be intense as can be seen in the movie Wolf of Wall Street (a movie that contains the best phone prospecting speech ever. That speech by the way should be watched frequently by anyone whose income depends on the ability to sell over the phone).

Outside B2B Sales

This book is dedicated to people whose job is to prospect, build a connection, qualify (investigate), present and close business accounts. Although knowledge from all the other categories of selling can be helpful when selling new accounts; Outside B2B Selling is it's own animal. Many Outside B2B Sales jobs include a territory or a prospect list that the Account Executive(AE) is able to manage and sell into exclusively. This keeps the other AEs from fighting over accounts for the most part.

Economic downturns can affect an outside AE but it is easier to survive than the inside retail salesperson because the outside AE can easily shift to other prospects who are in less affected industries. However, Outside AE's have a lot of competition and the buyers for many companies are trained to make an Outside AE's life difficult so the environment can be hostile. The key to success as an Outside AE has to be intense about prospecting, be able to overcome rejection and be tenacious about closing business.

Every company will have some sort of training for new AEs unfortunately that training typically is convoluted and softened by people trained in human resources that couldn't sell a bottle of water on an ocean beach when it is 115 degrees out. So this book will contain some harsh language and some hard truths that a new AE might never be told but could be fired for not knowing. One or two of the suggestions in this book could seem a little shady - but the intent here is to help the readers make the most money possible as fast as possible and to survive and thrive in his or her business as a hunter of new business accounts.

Chapter Two

Getting Started as fast as possible so you can start earning commissions

In the beginning of most jobs there is a training period. Your goal should be 1. Absorb the training they do give you as deeply as possible and 2. Get through it as fast as possible so you can go out and start making sales.

Most training systems allow a new employee enough time to consume the material at a leisurely pace and don't put any sales expectations on him or her. Rather than moseying through the material, it is better to complete it as fast as possible and then start making calls. Even if some of the calls get screwed up you can chalk it up to being a new guy or gal. Prospects forget your mistakes and your employer will not fault you for getting out there and hustling without delay.

In order to absorb the training, I recommend using the SQ3R method of study. SQ3R stands for Survey, Question, Read and Recite. How it works is:

Survey: Read headings in all the material.

Question: Write down questions as you survey about the material. They can be any questions.

Read: Read front to back.

Read a second time: This time scan it to answer your questions.

Recite: Because you are in sales you will need to talk about the information and it also helps you to remember if you hear it. Read outloud all the headings, the questions you had and the answers you found.

Using this method you will not only learn the material but you will memorize a lot of the finer detail that a lot of the veterans in your company will have forgotten or never picked up on in the first place. This method will take a little more time and a lot more concentration than most people give to training but it will be worth every minute when you get out in the field.

Regardless of the company's training there are some universal things you need to know well as an outside AE. They are company information, product information and service information.

Company

Learn the company origin story. Their founder's name, his or her hokey dokey story of how he started and then how the business blew up to the mega presence they now have. No matter how this story is presented to you pull out your notebook and break it down into these bullet points:

- Name of founder/s

- Original idea

- What caused that idea to grow or if your company is newer why the founder expects it to grow in the future.

- One or two surprising details - there is usually some unusual fact in a company's background. Save a couple of these nuggets to make your future prospects say wow! or laugh.

- Annual revenue It helps your prospect know that you aren't fly by night if you can tell your company's annual revenue. A big number is like a referral because obviously, your company gets its revenue from sales to customers like the one you are talking to. Other people in your prospect's shoes have said yes.

- List of important customers and a note about what they produce, who their customers are and how your company really makes a difference for them.

If you can easily list off those 6 points, you will be doing better than most other people in the company and you will add a lot of credibility to what you do in the eyes of your colleagues, prospects, family and friends. Do not underestimate the value of the company story. People will enjoy hearing about it is an instant rapport builder for prospects.

Product

First of all a product can be a concept as in advertising, distribution from a catalog of standard parts, projects that involve many moving parts or simply a thing. AE's should think of the product as the thing that the customer ends up with; the thing that they will say they bought or contracted.

It is not important to be an expert in all of the fine details of your product (whatever it is) before you get out selling. You should work on obtaining product mastery but don't sweat product ignorance in the beginning even though your engineers, service managers or other know-it-alls will tell you that the product you sell is too complex for an ordinary person to present without months of arduous training. Learn these points before you call prospects solo:

- What is it supposed to do for the customer? (Make bullet points)

- Why would the customer benefit from the product? (More bullet points)

- What makes the product better than competing products? Can that be visually proven somehow?

- What are available upgrades? Why would the customer benefit from upgrading right away?

- What are the defects that customers might not like? Is there a way to position those in a good light?

- How can you physically demonstrate the product.

Going through the exercise of learning those 6 points, writing them down and practice saying them out loud will make you seem like an expert to an outsider. That's enough to get going with your sales job and start making money. All the minutia will come through your customer questions anyway. If a customer asks about some detail that you don't know you can always say you will have to look into that and then schedule a follow up meeting, phone call or Skype to talk about that point and other things like moving forward with the sale.

Service

Understanding the service side of any business is important. The service team will often create a lot of havoc for an AE. Most of this havoc however, can be avoided if the AE communicates to the service team in a way that they understand. Knowing how to communicate with them means understanding how they function. Here are some points to understand:

What kind of paperwork do they need? Detail is important but try to follow the paperwork through their systems and ask about things that piss them off. These things typically are easy to avoid if you know and for some reason companies do not typically spend enough time going over contracts, job orders, shipping requests and etc. It is best to talk to the people processing paperwork and filling orders to get a good understanding of paperwork.

- How are ETAs determined? How can you track orders in the system? What are typical order times (from approval to delivery)?

- What causes delays?

- In a pinch what can be done to get orders rushed? Ideally you will be able to figure a way to get all of your orders rushed merely by putting your name on them.

Who is the dumbass? In every company I have ever visited there is a dumbass or sometimes a series of dumbasses. You can tell who they are by listening to what they say. They will give a lot of excuses and be very defensive. These are people to be prepared for. They will make your life difficult and your customers pissed. Discreetly ask other AEs about the dumbass and find out if there are ways to bypass him or her or them. If you have to work with the dumbass or dumbasses then cc everything to his or her boss and your own boss. It is not fun being that guy but if you are consistent the dumbass or dumbasses might give your projects more attention. Also these are the people to give little gifts to. Make them feel like you really respect their loathsome asses.

Finally, before you go out and sell you have to address the fact that you are a clown that nobody (except other clowns) is going to take serious. You will have to spend a little time getting ready to overcome that little nugget in chapter 3.

READ CHAPTER 3 BEFORE YOU ENGAGE YOUR PROSPECTS IF POSSIBLE.

Chapter Three

Your story: It's acting

Famous actors know the importance of creating a persona. The audience comes to expect a certain sort of portrayal of a character when they go to see a movie with Jack Black or Kevin Costner. Unlike actors we don't need to appear in several roles. Who cares if we get typecast?

We are always salespeople representing whatever kind of product or service our employers want to push. So we should spend a long time developing our roles.

The following are just some of the areas we should pay close attention to when developing our sales persona.

Your uniform

There is a good chance that your prospects see 5 or more salespeople every week and for the most part they dress and look pretty similar. When your prospect sees you she might be trying to remember which one you are. The harder she has to think about it the less rapport you two share. McDonald's, FedEx, and just about every other giant company whose employees have limited but repeat contact with customers figured this out a long time ago and that is why they dress them all in uniforms.

Account Executives typically shiver at the thought of wearing a uniform and that makes sense. We don't want the customer thinking of us as so unsophisticated that we can't dress ourselves. However, we really should be so sophisticated that we dress in a uniform of our own making to build rapport with our prospect faster. That means instead of wearing a different zany tie every day guys should pick a couple of colors of ties (preferably colors that are in the company they work for's logo). Ladies should stay away from too much variety as well. Don't wear sequins one day and a dark cotton blazer the next day. If a lady outside AE wants to wear sequins, then she should wear them every day. Regardless of sex - pick a style and few colors and dress that way every day.

Pick a good hairstyle and wear it like that every day keeping it well trimmed, dyed, permed or whatever your preference. It is not so important what kind of style that you choose as is that it looks pretty much the same every time.

Beards should be worn all the time or not at all. A lot of men who have beards seem to believe that having a beard means they don't have to shave. These men look like pigs and I would never buy anything from them. If you are going to wear a beard in outside sales then it has to be shaped, trimmed daily and enhance your appearance. If you cannot commit to keeping your beard looking combed and perfect every day, then don't wear a beard at all. That goes for the stubbly look too. The stubbly look makes guys look like they are fun at parties but stupid at business.

Other than your appearance, you might try to figure some catch phrases. Using catch phrases help to identify you as a character and that helps build rapport as well. It doesn't have to be a single tired line but if you find one that is really good - use it and keep using it. People will do impressions of you and that is a good thing. It's all part of being knowable and known. A really good example of someone developing and then using a catch phrase is on the USA legal drama Suits. The character Lewis Litt spends time talking into a voice recorder trying different catchphrase. The one he landed on that was perfect is, "You just got Litt up!" Corny? Yes. Memorable? Definitely. One word of advice on catch phrases - once you commit - don't quit. The longer you keep it around the more people will remember it.

Your story

Every AE needs a story to tell customers about themselves. It should be equal parts true, relevant and legendary. The best way to start building your story is to answer these questions on paper:

- How did you find yourself working for the company you are at now?

- What do you think the company liked about you.

- What do you love about the company?

- Add one story about a challenge that you overcame.

- What is your mission in life?

Now here is an example of personal story creation:

I got hired after college.

I grew up in the area that the territory was in.

I love the secretaries that answer the phones.

When I was a young manager the GM plant in my town closed down. The massive loss of business that year from GM and all the accounts that supported GM made my job very tough. I had to work with companies of every industry plan their downsizing. Some of those companies that hadn't prepared went out of business. Others survived by adjusting their business model to live in a world without GM. Then at the end of that year which was the most challenging of my career my position changed to a Route Sales role. At the time, I was hurt because while I had worked so hard and saved many accounts the quarterly losses were just too much for my managers. Even though I was embarrassed, I was grateful to not be unemployed like so many of the people in my town.

As a Route Sales Representative, I found that I really *liked helping people work through their issues so in a small way I could help them be prepared in case a terrible situation ever came up against their business. I was soon promoted to an Account Executive where I thrived selling new business only.*

I want to be able to buy nice things for *my family and myself.*

Taking those elements that are all true, next I show *their relevance:*

My education is based on the cutting edge and is *more advanced than my competitors.*

Because of my familiarity with this region especially the people, *I know better what is in my client's best interests than some slick Willy from the big city.*

The people that I work with are some of the *best people I have ever known and our entire team is devoted to making sure our customers are happy.*

Seeing how some businesses survived - even in a reduced capacity and others had to go out of business really taught me that making good decisions is not just important but absolutely vital. Helping my clients make good decisions is what drives me in this job and I am proud to say that I have helped hundreds of businesses like yours by reducing operational costs, improving customer perception and I even help to reduce workplace accidents - the kind that cost businesses like yours millions of dollars a year.

I will do anything it takes to make my customers happy because when it boils down to it - I am a people pleaser. I can't be happy unless you are too.

Next, we just add a little legend to our story to give it flavor and our story is complete.

In college, I studied a lot of companies in your exact industry in fact I heavily considered working in your industry instead of the one I am in. (Showing I am almost an expert and I appreciate the various elements of what they do. It doesn't matter if it's not exactly true. It is flattering to my prospect because he or she did in fact choose that industry.)

I probably went to school with a lot of your employees. (very unlikely)

We actually pay our service people the most in our industry. That way we can recruit the best and brightest and keep them working with us for decades. People don't quit when they start working with us. (Every company has to deal with some turnover and every company has a few jackasses.)

I know for a fact that I made the difference in some companies of whether they survived or died. One thing that I have proven to myself is that I am good for business. (Most salespeople cannot say that they saved someone else's business from shutting down. Then again, maybe they could say that.)

I have been called at 2:00 am because one of my customers ran out of product and he couldn't get a hold of anyone else. He almost had to stop production which would have been very expensive with his 120 third shift employees on the clock. I got my clothes on and made the delivery myself because - what is more important? My sleep or my customer's business? I know the answer to that question is my customer's business every time.

After going through that exercise, you should write out your personal story as one long flowing story and then condense it. Then condense it into bullet points that you can use on the phone later. You won't ever use all of the points on the phone but it is good to have it ready. By telling the same story repeatedly, it becomes easier and more convincing. I highly recommend using the personal story as part of every first time meeting.

Social Media

One last point - Social Media matters! Go through your social media posts on all sites and get rid of items that make you look stupid. You should have more pictures of other people than selfies. Understand that every single post on every single social media site is going to be viewed by your prospects. Going forward, post positive things only.

This is sales and you are very big part of the product you are selling. You can have fun with this as long as you can commit to the character that you design. Don't be an accidental character known for bad breath, wrinkled clothes and poor follow through. Come up with scripts and use them. Write down your character outline and commit to the part.

Chapter 4

Your first week in your territory

It is my opinion that any outside AE should spend the first week in their territory. Better yet would be to spend the first four weeks prospecting door to door in his or her territory to get to see what opportunities are out there. I would spend Fridays on the phone only calling the prospects (where there might be opportunity) met during the week.

Start earlier than necessary and stay later than you want to.

An important difference between the sales champions and the salespeople who get their asses canned and have to go back to scrubbing out the grease traps at Taco Bell boils down to one thing - endurance. If you want to kick ass, then you have to get up early and get moving. A lot of authors suggest getting up an hour earlier than you have to to get your mind set for the day. I think that's good advice but when that hour is over; get out the door looking sharp and get to your territory where business is already happening. If your boss says to start at 8 then get there at 6. If he says 9 then get there at 6 and if he says 6, then you better be there at 4 am because some other AE who is hungrier than you is going to get out their first and take your sale and then it is back to the grease traps.

When you get to the field, then look around for the types of companies that should do business with you. Walk in the door - even the back door if the front is locked. Walk in like it's normal and ask about the product or service you sell. If it is janitorial supplies, ask where they keep them and see if you can find out who is in charge. You might end up having a first time meeting right away and that would be good. More likely, you'll get someone's name and contact information (ask for the direct line and email address too). You definitely want to find out what they have (that you sell) and who they are getting it from. When you leave and have written down your notes, then immediately go to the next prospect. The next prospect should be as close to the first one as possible. The more you see the stronger of an AE you will become. It's like weight lifting.

Lunch should not be more than 30 minutes. Stay off the internet. Your goal is quantity of in person prospecting calls and you can't have high quantity doing a bunch of internet research so it's best to just leave the phone in the glove box all day.

Around 3pm AE's start to get tired and want to go home. Resist that urge at all costs. Prospects are working hard until 5pm and beyond. AE's should work until 5 as well even though they can get away with leaving earlier.

Keep prospecting

Every day for as many as your manager will let you, go out and prospect morning to night. This is training and getting yourself used to hustling. If you go soft, you'll make less money in the future and that would suck.

Keep track of every prospect (name, contact, contact info, current service provider or supplier) in a small notebook. Don't carry in a binder full of neat slides unless you absolutely have to. Prospecting is about learning where the opportunities are. If you need your binder you can always go back out to the car. Otherwise, just a small pocket sized notebook, a pen and business card is fine.

At the end of each day, take a moment to tally the number of prospects you visited each day. Compete with yourself each day to get the highest number you can. Superstar AE's typically double the first day's prospecting call numbers on the 4th day.

Contact Relationship Management (CRM) Logging

Most companies will have some sort of CRM software that they will want you to log all of your activity into. Take a few minutes each night to log all of the activity you did while the memories are still fresh. Use abbreviations to make it fast, but get it done. The bosses will want to see evidence of your hard work and this is where they will look. Plus you will want to follow up on these prospects later and get a meeting with them. Any inside info that you can look at later will help.

Chapter Five

The Phone

When I first started working as an AE the scariest thing to me about my new job was for some reason the phone. I was much more comfortable working with prospects face to face. People were usually nice to me even when I babbled or got stumped on a question. As I have talked to more AE's both tenured and new I have learned that I was not alone in my apprehension to prospect on the phone. I am not sure why this fear exists but it most certainly does so we have to plan to deal with and overcome it.

Keep Score

There is a tendency to get distracted when sitting down to make phone calls. Whether it be from fear, stress or because you have the attention span of a three year old doesn't matter. Every AE I know gets distracted and will go a whole hour and make only 5 phone calls - or less.

You have to get past distractions. I suggest keeping score in ten minute increments. Every time you dial make a hash mark on a piece of paper. Every time you set an appointment put a hash mark on the other side. Every 10 minutes tally it, circle it and start again. If 10 minutes passes and you only made 1 call - you might suck and need to focus. At the end of 10 minutes instead of going to get a cup of coffee, you might dial one more time just to beat your score.

Your dials are like yards gained in a football game but your appointments set are your touchdowns. You have to be able to stay on task and keep dialing but if you can't get any appointments then you need to hit the weight room. Salespeople train by reading books like this, rehearsing call scripts, trying new plays, working on vocal tonation, pitch and cadence. If we want to make more touchdowns we have to train more - just like any other sport. That is why I break my scoring down to 10 minute increments. It works.

I found 10 minutes to be my personal sweet spot. When I was first experimenting with this strategy I used an hour but I got too bored with that so 10 minutes it became. Also - I have a form I created and use. If you would like it - feel free to email me at jim.zimmerman@outlook.com and I will send it to you in excel format.

Talking to the Gatekeeper

First Thing we need to do is plan for what we will say when we are talking to the gatekeeper (the person who screens your phone calls), your contact, and what to say on voicemail.

Gatekeeper: The best words you can use here are "Can you help me?". The phrase can you help me elicits the person on the other end of the phone call's compassion as a fellow human being talking to another human being. It can help to bypass her automatic response to say, "He's in a meeting. I can give you to his voicemail."

An example:

Gatekeeper: "Thank you for calling Morningside Daisy Corporation; This is Lizzie Borden. How can I help you today?

AE: Hi Lizzie, this is Nick Butler with C.E.I.P. I am wondering if you could help me. I am new to my company and am wondering if your firm could use the kind of (whatever products or services you sell) my firm offers to companies like yours but I am afraid I don't know where to start. Can you help me?

Gatekeeper: I can try.

AE: First of all do you know if your company uses (whatever it is you are selling)?

Gatekeeper: I am not sure. I think Margaret Sanger in H.R. oversees that but she's out to lunch. Do you want me to put you in her voicemail?

AE: Actually, I don't want to leave a big long message - would you be able to give me her email address and maybe her direct line so I could check back with her later today?

Gatekeeper: Sure. Let me find her card.

Make sure to convey gratitude and write down her name so you can remind her of your previous conversation when she was so helpful. Remembering gatekeeper's names and any details may seem tedious but it does help. If you are extra ambitious - send her a thank you note with your business card.

Not all conversations with gatekeepers will go as smoothly but a lot of them will. Sometimes during this exchange the gatekeeper will say, "Oh wait. She just got off the phone - I will transfer you now."

Now let's take a look at what to say when you are talking to the the decision maker (DM)

Example:

    DM: Hi this is Jack.

    AE: Hi Jack. This is Nick Butler with C.E.I.P. and I reduced several of your competitors' overhead and expenses and helped them to drastically improve their production efficiency using a cutting edge solution that was developed by my company. I have not had a chance to meet with you yet but I am going to be in your area on the 14th and I would like to stop and visit with you and see what your current process looks like. Do you have any time at 2:00 on Tuesday the 14th?

    DM: Can you just send me something?

    AE: Well, what we do is rather proprietary and we try not to pass out our business model to anybody who isn't going to partner with us. The environment is just to competitive. I am sure you can understand that; right?

    DM: Ok. I can meet with you at 2 on the 14th but I really only can give you an hour. Is that ok?

    AE: That will work perfectly. I will see you then. Lizzie gave me your email address - so I'll just send you over a quick confirmation with my contact information in case anything comes up. I look forward to meeting you.

    If your company has a script for you to use - I would use it a lot but make sure that it meets these criteria:

Executive Presence

    You need to sound like an executive with a bit of business sense. Managers aren't sitting around waiting to talk to salespeople but they do like talking about business. Frame your product or solution in a way that demonstrates your professionalism. In the above example Nick speaks the manager's language by addressing overhead, expenses and production efficiency. Be prepared to talk briefly about how your product or solution addresses these areas if you mention them.

If you can't think of how your product or service addresses the business needs of your prospect - success will be hard to acquire.

Competitive Advantage

Suggesting that your prospect's competitors are at an advantage over them because they deal with you may be the thorn that gets their ears to perk up and pay attention to you. Nobody wants to be at a disadvantage in business. If you can't name a competitor than try to make him or her the first one that has an advantage over his or her competition.

Warning - people tend to be more motivated from fear than desire. Talking about his or her competitors who do use your service is stronger than offering him or her the opportunity to be first.

Built Around the Close
This might seem obvious but before you dial you need to have a very specific idea of what the mission is. For most outside AE's the mission is to get a meeting with the prospect. If you can't set the appointment at least be prepared to ask some useful questions like - Are you currently using a service or buying a product like mine? Which of my competitors are you purchasing from? Are you under contract and if so when will you be revisiting it? Planning your attack prior to making the call is absolutely critical and half the AE's I listen to obviously do not have a plan.

Backup Plan

Most calls will contain at least one objection to meeting with you. Some objections might make it better to just hang up and call someone else. If they are currently in the first month of a 5 year contract with your competitor; it probably doesn't make sense spending a ton of time meeting and showing how awesome you, your company and your products are. They can't buy so it's a waste of time; you are better off scheduling yourself to call them in a couple years and dialing the next number.

What if they can buy, but don't want to meet with you? That is where you need to have some good backups to counter with and get the appointment anyway. Warning - Never underestimate this. Never skip it. Don't be a coward. If you get good at turning around the no's you will get business that a lesser AE would totally miss out on. Here are some examples of common rejections and turnarounds.

Example:

Prospect: We are very happy with our current provider.

AE: That's really great news! Our customers are extremely loyal to us too. The only difference is a lot of our customers pay 30 - 40% less than our competitors charge. I do think it would be worth taking a look at a way to have good service and at the same time save a lot of money that could be used elsewhere. Are you available next Tuesday at 2PM? (At this point just be quiet. Most times you'll hear him or her digging through his schedule and you will get the appointment)

Prospect: We don't use those types of services (or products)?

AE: Yeah, that's exactly why I called. I thought it was funny that your company wasn't using (whatever I sell). Companies that use us operate more efficiently and see a marked reduction in employee and customer turnover. The kind of impact that we can bring to (their company name) could be significant. Are you available for me to come visit with you next Tuesday at 2PM?

Concise

Attention is a fleeting thing and there is a strong chance that your prospect is not waiting for salespeople to call her. More likely, she is right in the middle of something and she was kind enough to pause so that she could answer the phone. If you cannot convey the majority of your message in 20 seconds you will lose credibility and become a nuisance.

Phone work is important but you will create negative progress if your prospect thinks you are annoying. If you call on the same prospect more than once and stumble along without reaching a point; the prospect will remember you and screen your calls. Instead of scoring the meeting you will have eliminated the phone as a source of contact for this prospect.

If you do happen to get on a prospect's nerves and ruin your phone chances - you need to switch strategies to other medias or a direct unscheduled visit.

So, how do you show Executive Presence, demonstrate a competitive advantage and be prepared to close in ten seconds? The answer is to front load your script and stick to it.

Start with a power statement to introduce yourself and then use a persuasive closing statement.

Example:

AE: Mr. Rogers, this Jim Zimmerman calling from V.S.C. Companies. I work with your competitor to reduce operating expenses. I am going to be in your area on the 19th of May and I would like to visit with you to show you some examples of how I helped your competitors and to see what I can do for you - are you available at 9:30 on May 19th?

If he says - I'm not interested - I can respond with anything just to ask again. It almost doesn't matter what I say to the objection. Many prospects are so programmed to saying no the response is automatic. You have to ask again.

My response to I'm not interested: Mr. Rogers, when I was at Harvard Business School I learned a pretty profound fact about business. Do you know what that is? The idea of business is to make profit - as much as possible. What I do is help reduce expenses for businesses like yours. In fact I have already helped your competitors reduce their expenses. Less expenses means more profit; right? Since, I am already planning on being in your area anyway on the 19th do you think we could just plan to meet at 9:30?

If you can get a prospect to stay on the phone with you long enough to go through a couple requests at least 50% of the time you will get the appointment. Most new sales people are too cowardly to get past the first no. You have to have courage and tenacity to succeed selling b2b.

Remember - the goal of most outside B2B salespeople on the phone is to set the appointment. If you can't set the appointment now then set it for later. If they don't want to look at their calendar then get their email and tell them you will send over a calendar invite.

Voicemail

One final note about phone calls - more than half the time you will get voicemail. If you leave a voicemail - tell the person something to entice them. If you have their email - send them one saying whatever you said on the voicemail. I recommend having a set plan for every single voicemail you leave and just leave the same one all day long. Tomorrow; set a different plan to leave on voicemail. Your emails can be copy and pasted into the body and boom - gone.

Monday Voicemail (Example):Hey Miss Junge I want to meet with you on the 21st when I will be in the area because I am showing another company on your street some of the benefits of having automated floor sweepers on shop floors to reduce debris, trip hazards and labor. I am going to email you over a calendar invite for the morning but if that doesn't work - please let me know what time that day does work for you. If you would like to call me back instead - my phone number is 555-123-4567.

Then send the email that says the same thing with a calendar invite attached and then dial the next number. This trick does work more than you would expect.

Chapter 6

The First Meeting

In your first meeting your goal is to appraise the prospect of its total value, determine who the other players are, find out who makes the decision, when they will make the decision and you want to identify points to build your presentation on. You also need to solidify a next step.

NOTE: Always be prepared to sell the business in the first meeting. It doesn't happen a lot but it does. Have agreements, order forms, or whatever you use to turn prospects into customers with you at all times.

Your approach

From the moment you walk to the door, keep your eyes open. What relevant observations can you make? Depending on what you sell - you may see opportunity before the meeting even starts so pay attention.

The secretary matters

Introduce yourself and it doesn't hurt to be a little playful. Smile. Comment on desk decor. Use eye contact. Don't overdo it or he might think you are a pain in the ass. Your goal is to make a positive first impression.

Hint: A little treat is usually appreciated. Give the secretary a candybar every time you see her and she will think you're one hell of a sweet salesperson.

Sit right

You want the people in the company to think you are intelligent and focussed on their business. Here is a list of things not to do in the client's waiting room:

DO NOT:

Play with your phone

Don't even check your email. Especially don't take a call in the waiting room. Better yet - leave your phone in the car.

Read their magazines

They are there for customers and you ain't one. Plus you are telling them you are bored.

Talk to other salespeople

In fact during working hours it's a good idea not to chit chat with people who can't buy from you, won't buy from you and who don't have influence. Networking is fine but it is just stupid to do it in a prospect's waiting room.

Don't fidget

Keep your hands mostly still. Don't kick your toe nervously. Try to imagine that you are the President of the president of your company. Presidents don't fidget.

Go through your Powerpoint slides

The waiting room is not the place to whip it out. You can mentally go through the slides without looking at them unless you have terrible short term memory. If you have terrible short term memory then both you and your prospect will be surprised by your slides.

Your goal in the first meeting is to make an excellent first impression here so behave like an executive not a high school kid.

When you finally get in to the meeting room resist the temptation to blather. Your goals are to appraise, discover, and plan. Your goal is not to present until the right time.

Your goals are to appraise, discover, and plan. Your goal is not to present until the right time.

You do have to share some information so here is where you tell the sales story (hopefully shorter than 60 seconds) from Chapter 3. You don't have to give them the whole thing verbatim but make sure it tells a story of who the hell you are and why you do what you do and what your company can do for the prospect. After you tell your story you are done telling. Start investigating.

Asking questions to keep the prospect telling is key. Information that will be useful are:

- Prospect background and philosophy about business.

- Example questions:

- How long have you been here? Always in this position?

- How did you get into this line of work?

- I know what your company does but what would you say makes it better than your competitors?

   NOTE: I would not recommend writing this stuff down because it will throw off the conversational tone. I do recommend writing it down immediately when you get in your car.

- Who actually makes the decision? At every meeting you should ask 1. Who else is involved in the decision making process and will I be able to present to him,her or them as well?

- What is their current process for handling whatever your solution is?

Example Questions:

- How do you currently handle _____?

- How does delivery work?

- What are the most important aspects of _____?

- Has there been any difficulty reaching those aspects?

- When _____ doesn't meet your requirements how does that affect your time? How about your employee's time.

- When was the last time that happened?

- Do you think if you were running [your competitor]'s business you could improve on their consistency and ability to meet your specs? How would you do that? (the response to that question is important and you should follow it with, "Yeah - that sounds pretty simple; doesn't it?")

NOTE: You do want to write down notes during this part of the meeting even if it happens during a tour of the facility.

You can go through these series of questions multiple times during your meeting but don't be robotic about it. The answers to each are very important to your presentation.

Locking it down:

Finally, you need to be prepared to set up the next meeting or write the contract then and there. Either way just tell the prospect that based on what you learned today you think that he or she might really like how your company does business and what you have to offer. Then ask if you can set up a follow up meeting on a specific date. Don't leave without landing on the calendar first or you're dead.

If their need is very current move ahead to the canned presentation of whatever you sell. Explain the process and timeline of delivery, installation and etc and Whip out the contract and get it signed.

After you have set the next appointment, be sure to shake hands, say bye to the prospect and the secretary and leave. The moment you get to your car, write your notes down and then quickly outline your draft presentation in your notebook. This habit will make your presentation better and also provide you with a list of tasks to do prior to the presentation.

Chapter Seven

Presentations

If you are using Powerpoint slides here are some rules:

Any page that isn't *100% crucial* to the specific prospect should be deleted. I'm serious. If you can't say for sure that your prospect will be interested in the information on a slide then don't present it. How do you know? You asked good questions and listened to the answers in the first meeting.

The first page after the cover page should describe their current situation in bullet point form. It should not be negative but opportunities to improve (that directly benefit your solution) should be mentioned.

The next slide should describe your specific operation, service and anything that would matter about your company to the prospect. It would be smart to, if you can describe a point or two about how your company avoids problems that your prospect cares about.

The next slide/s should describe each product or service specifically. If you want to sell them 20 things from your catalog - you should probably have 20 pages unless the things are similar enough to batch them. Go over the features on the slide and at the bottom answer the question of why it will matter to the prospect. When you are presenting - only talk about why it matters and give some basic context.

If you have products to demonstrate - demonstrate them when the slides come up for that specific product.

The next slide should describe process in a little more detail.

The next slide will have the price.

Finally, have a page that describes terms.

After you have completed your PowerPoint ask if your prospect is prepared to go ahead now. If he or she is not - then you need to get on the calendar. Say something like, "I would like to follow up next week when I will be in the area on Tuesday. Is that enough time to decide if I stop by at 11 next Tuesday?" **If you fail to get a commitment for the follow up - you will most likely not get the sale.** Put a deadline to make the decision on your prospect and it will be urgent otherwise it will go to the bottom of the pile.

Make the presentation for people who are not there. Earlier I mentioned that you would list the feature of every product but only talk about the benefit. Your whole PowerPoint has to be made for people who are not in the room to be able to go through it and understand it. Don't read it because your prospect will be bored and hate you. Just present what you want and skip what you can.

Add credibility when you can. Use quotations, reference letters from enthusiastic customers, logos from well known customers, legal mentions that support the use of your product or service. You can also add any awards you or your company have achieved. Don't overdo it but remember - you are asking this prospect to gamble on you. You can put his mind at ease by showing how others who gambled on you in the past came out winners.

Your presentation is probably the part of selling that is most fun. It is your chance to perform; just remember not to get too caught up in your own performance that your attention drifts from your target. If he looks bored stop the presentation and ask a couple questions to wake his mind up. If he knows about the product - it's ok to skim a little faster. If he leans in or looks otherwise interested slow it down and try to get him to engage. The difference between a rookie and a tenured AE is most often their comfort in the presentation and their ability to read their prospect and adjust as needed. For you - it will be something to work on. Just make sure at the end you always take the sale.

Chapter Eight

Taking the sale

Always ask or assume the close - even if it seems like the prospect is leaning towards no. Don't ever assume failure. If it is no - then you have to make the prospect say so by asking him for a commitment and waiting for the answer.

If you did your investigation, customization and presentation correctly then your prospect should want your offering. It is pretty rare for one to say - "Yeah! Wow! This is great - sign me up! Now!!!!" More likely, they will sit there as if in deep thought. In actuality they might be in deep thought - more likely they are stupefied and will need you to guide them to the next logical action. The best way that I have found to take the prospect to the next logical action is to say if that all sounded good - then all I need is a signature here and I put the paperwork (that I did in advance) in front of her and point at the line to sign on.

Dealing with Fear

This is an area you can expect some pushback. People are afraid of making mistakes so you need to anticipate (and bring up before them if possible) the items that customers are most often afraid of. If you have an agreement then be prepared to show how the paperwork actually protects them in case they are unsatisfied, want to quit/ cancel.

A sentence that I was fond of using is, "Listen, we have plenty of customers who love us and that is what we want BUT if you don't want to do business with us we prefer to be able to come get our stuff, shake hands and leave friends. Maybe, if we are that bad; we just have some kinks to work out and your leaving is exactly the wake up call we need. I don't know because it doesn't come up that often. I mean this isn't rocket science. It is not actually that hard to service a company like yours perfectly. But if for whatever reason you want to quit - you can and it says that right here." I point. They look (but usually don't read) and then they sign.

Secret*: Business customers usually don't quit unless there is a big reason to quit. Just like it was hard to get the initial appointment it takes a while for them to get mad enough to start dealing with alternative salespeople. You just want to give them peace of mind and then follow it up with doing everything you can do to make sure their service and product is perfect.*

When you encounter fear during the sale, you have to be able to handle it smartly. Try to think about all of the possible ways you would be feeling if you were in the prospect's shoes and plan how to council past those fears and practice. When it comes up in a meeting after you have responded, ask for the sale again.

Ask for it again - don't feel guilty. After my speech about the ease of breaking out of contract, I always ask if that makes sense and then hand them my pen and point to the signature line and then - they sign it.

Sometimes they say no. Sometimes they say they have to talk it over with others. Most often - they say yes. If that isn't the case most times with your experience then you should probably examine where you are consistently failing and adjust.

Hint: *If you are an extrovert it you are probably failing in the investigation phase and if you are an introvert you are probably failing in presentation and overcoming objections. Wherever your failing at - work hard at fixing it and you will be amazed.*

Chapter Nine

Paperwork

Turning it in

There are two types of AEs that work for Sales Managers. Producers and idiots. Producers don't take much management. They go out and sell. When they are done selling, they turn in their paperwork complete every time. Their paperwork includes all the details they discussed with the customer so everyone else in the company knows what is expected. Producers don't make excuses and they most often would get offended if questioned because they know how to wipe their own asses.

The other type of AEs are the ones that Sales Managers have to spend all their time on repeating instructions, asking for paperwork, asking why paperwork is incomplete, having to fix their screw ups and calling the customer to apologize. If your Sales Manager is bugging the crap out of you - then my friend, he thinks you are an idiot. So stop being an idiot by:

- Paperwork has to be complete.

- All signatures have to be on the paperwork

- Every item you promised has to be on the paperwork. Your service, delivery, order entry people are not mind readers. Write it down BEFORE you turn it in.

- If you need money up front - make sure you turn that in exactly in conjunction with your procedures.

- Any cover page documentation that your company requires has to be filled out regardless of its tediousness.

- Update your CRM software immediately showing the prospect as a sold opportunity so your bosses will know.

- Any weekly, monthly, or quarterly reports should be done BEFORE your boss asks. Set a reminder for yourself that is hours earlier than when she wants it and get it turned in.

- Any time you can get something done before your boss asks you are doing yourself a favor. Stay out of his mind and just go out and sell.

Checkup Reminders
PUT THESE REMINDERS IN YOUR CALENDAR

In a pure hunter role we are instructed to sell and forget. Let the others in the company do their job. That is what you should do except these 2 checkups:

1. Checkup on your people to ensure delivery. installation is on schedule. If not - you need to call the prospect and let him or her know even if someone else already called. Don't let the customer feel like you are a liar that doesn't care. You want a good reputation.

2. Checkup with the customer after installation or delivery to make sure the customer is happy.

   BONUS: Call your customer every 3 - 6 months just to ask them how the hell they are doing. Every once in a while one of these calls will turn into an opportunity that you won't expect. If your sales role also has a farming component you will want to call way more frequently than every 6 months.

3. Find the people who can but won't and invent workarounds

   Way back in Chapter 2 under the Service section we talked about the dumbass. Working with dumbasses is like fighting martial arts. Sometimes you need karate which deals with attacks directly other times you need judo which deals with understanding your opponent and using their momentum to achieve your desired result. Sometimes there are ways to just sidestep and avoid the dumbass altogether. Each situation is unique but I recommend having plans for all three strategies and be ready to employ them for every sale.

Examples:

   Use judo - After encountering a person that complains about every sale and drags their feet - find out what they do and turn in your sales with their work mostly complete. This is a pain in the ass but sometimes it is the correct strategy.

   Use karate - Start turning in date stamped and scanned versions of your paperwork and CC'ing their boss/es. Then set reminders to follow up on everything with them and each time you do CC their boss/es. Be courteous and short. Don't explain why you are following up. Explaining anything to these assholes will just piss them off and make them work even harder against you in the future. If you are asked - just say you are a huge believer in being thorough.

   Sidestep - Sometimes there are ways to avoid dumbasses altogether by going to someone else. Do that. WARNING: This may be against the rules and you do not want the better person to complain about you. Gifts, complimentary conversation, thank you (verbal and in notes) and whatever you can do to deepen your relationship with the workaround are vitally important.

Chapter Ten

Maximizing commission and results

In the beginning new AE's are just trying to build momentum and don't typically think about strategizing in such a way to benefit themselves but that is probably a mistake. I recommend taking your commission plan home at night and developing scenarios where you will get paid the most and so that your reporting period makes you look like a superstar.

This is the game that salespeople have to play in order to get ahead. Benevolence in business is stupid and is not often rewarded. Don't think for a second that your integrity is such that you can skip this chapter. Remember management set up the reporting periods and commission structures they way they are to judge you. Promotions for salespeople that don't get paid well and have excellent quarters don't happen. They shouldn't. Salespeople are by nature in business for themselves and should be judged mainly by the numbers. Average performing but tenured AE's are passed up by young hotshots all the time. Tenure shouldn't count for anything. We are only as good as the last report and what we have closed for the next one.

Sandbagging

It is <u>not</u> cheating to sandbag

Sandbagging is the art of holding sales in order to hit in a way that benefits the salesperson most. An example is when a company holds a contest that starts in September and an AE makes a big sale the last week of August. If she holds it for one week it might result in her getting a free weekend vacation to Las Vegas. It would be completely stupid to turn that sale in in August and everybody around her would agree (secretly). Everyone remembers who went on the trip. Everyone thinks of that person as a winner. Everyone thinks the salespeople who didn't win are losers (by comparison). Does it make more sense in business to be thought of as a loser or a winner?

So, I strongly recommend sandbagging. Be discreet because if done to brazenly it can get you in trouble. Make sure you work with your prospect to let him know that you will be delivering a week (or whatever the needed time is) later than normal. You are a salesperson so this shouldn't be tough. Sell it.

If your sales are counted after delivery, you need to backwards plan when the account will bill. This is a little trickier because often there are a lot of wheels moving together to make delivery happen. Backorders can hurt and that dumbass mentioned in chapter 2 love to wreck salespeople's plans. You'll just have to get good at it.

Hint: Get customer support by making your best interests his or hers Offering sales to customers for taking deliver when it best suits you works nicely. They are pleasantly surprised and happy to take whatever discount or freebie that you can provide. It's fun to make up names for these sales too. I run Christmas specials, End of year specials, Tax Day Specials, and etc. Sometimes I get extra creative with things like birthday bonuses. It doesn't matter, I always have something in my back pocket to make the customer feel great about installing when it best suits me. I don't recommend pulling out these bonus ideas until after the customer has agreed to go with you. Otherwise you look a little used car salesmansy.

Make your quarter ASAP and then start working on the next

Another, important point here is sandbagging strategically. Sometimes there is no contest, no commission kicker (bonus for selling specific items or ways) but there is always a reporting period. Consistency is the key to Salesperson longevity. It is poor strategy to double your quota one period (quarter, month and etc) and follow it with a quarter that makes you look like garbage.

You should always be selling to hit your plan and once your plan is hit - then it's time to start focussing on the next quarter. If you think you can have two good quarters in a row with what you have in and what you have coming - then you're fine but you need to always be planning ahead.

How to plan a giant quarter to get promoted

How to plan a giant quarter to maximize career opportunity is a dirty little way to get promoted over the tenured AEs. Once you have learned and mastered the fine art of sandbagging there may come a time when you decide that you would like to apply for a bigger position. Hopefully, you can plan a quarter ahead of when you will do that because the best situation is to walk in to the interview with your boss with several strong quarters in your portfolio but the last quarter is just a bang up, holy shit quarter. Here you sandbag to have a decent quarter just prior the bang up one and you don't sandbag for the quarter afterwards.

Don't use this strategy often but when you are competing against a tenured salesperson for the same job and you are sitting on an astronomical quarter and had several good ones just prior you will pass that old dog with no problems. However, if you don't get the promotion - you will have to make your next quarter good and that means the same quarter that you are planning as your power blaster - you need to up your prospecting to a ridiculous level. That means working about 2 - 3 hours longer every day during that month and working harder.

Follow this plan of maximizing commissions and results and you will be loved by management and you will make more money. You may even get promoted. A foolish AE is one that disregards this chapter.

Chapter Eleven

Final thoughts

In this book I really only focussed on the hunting side of outside sales. There are a lot of b2b outside sales jobs out there and a lot of them also have a farming aspect to them. If your job is one of those - then I will just mention that you should divide your day to work on farming for a percentage and hunting for a percentage. Most AE's that farm can't hunt very well. True hunter AE's aren't always the best farmers either.

True hunters do it for the kill and once the sale is had they are hungry for the next one. Farmers are better at nurturing the customers and learn how to grow their internal business without having to do a lot of prospecting for new clients.

It is my feeling that the best solution is to divide your day or week completely so you are either in farm mode or hunting mode. That doesn't mean not to go try to sell a new business across the street after you visit one of your clients - do that every time. What it means is that you only call your current book of business from certain times every week and then work on new business only during the opposite periods every week.

Here is an example how that schedule could look:

AE Weekly Schedule Template

Monday	**Farming**	**6:00 - 12:00**
	Hunting	**12:30 - 5:00**
Tuesday	**Hunting**	**6:00 - 12:00**
	Farming	**12:30 - 5:00**
Wednesday	**Farming**	**6:00 - 12:00**
	Hunting	**12:30 - 5:00**
Thursday	**Hunting**	**6:00 - 12:00**
	Farming	**12:30 - 5:00**
Friday	**Farming**	**6:00 - 12:00**
	Hunting	**12:30 - 5:00**

Following this strategy will allow you to hit all of your prospects and clients during the week and grow your internal and new business. Play with your schedule how you like but you definitely need to keep the work of farming and hunting separated.

How long to work an outside sales job? If your job is hunter only - I recommend working any outside sales job for about 3 - 5 years in the same territory. If the company you work for doesn't expand your territory or your role - it is best to move on. The worst thing in the world for an AE is to be loyal to a company or product. We are communicators. We make business happen. Companies want us to make their business happen. If the company you work for doesn't have opportunities to grow then go find one that has more opportunities.

Don't get me wrong though - I don't think most AE's should be Sales Managers. Personally, I think Sales Management is a crap job. You get to play with spreadsheets, tell loser salespeople to get busy, try to sound smart in conference calls and useless meetings filled with other people that are also trying to sound smart. In the 21st century sales management has become an administrative job that has little to do with selling. So true sales hunters probably don't make for great sales managers.

We are the warriors meant to hunt and take business. We hear no far more than we hear yes and we keep on dialing. We are used to walking into businesses and are treated like dirt after our introduction. We make our way with bloody knuckles and bloody noses every single day - and we love it. The thrill of the kill makes the pain of the scratches and bruises disappear. When we hear other employees of the same company whine about how much we make as AE's - we internally swell up with pride and think, "Yeah, that's right mother fucker." We are superior to our supervisors. We are unlike any other person at any company that we work at. We are shape shifters; silver tongued devils. Without us our companies would die and nobody will ever admit that to you. Congratulations on joining us selling B2B.

About the Author

Growing up Wisconsin under the tutelage of his Grandfather Eugene Zimmerman an entrepreneur and philosopher in his own right James Zimmerman learned the ability to make transactions happen and to innovate new ways to provide people with the products, services and ideas that they wanted.

As a young man James worked in various forms of selling including selling manufactured homes and modular homes at a small retailer in Janesville Wisconsin where he built a sales program that more than doubled the sales of any previous year's volume in the company's half century of business. He did this by first creating systems of marketing and selling and then applying them to his team.

After leaving the housing industry he entered the textiles market where he made a name for himself selling business to business to small and large companies business to business (b2b). He was amazed at the difference between selling houses to retail prospects whose interest tended to be up to a whim. Business prospects had real needs that had to be filled in order to function and would absolutely purchase given the right opportunity to do so. He found that simply following a good process absolutely resulted in success. The level of success depended wholly on the amount of consistent effort put into that system.

The realization was so profound that he began to study B2B selling strategies from popular authors like Michael Weinberg, Mathew Dixon, Zig Ziglar and more. After years of fine tuning the process James decided to begin writing books that are complete yet concise in the delivery of the sales systems he uses.

He plans to in the future offer companies his method to quickly train people in the New to B2B process to get new hires out on the street and selling fast.

Watch for his next book in the New to B2B series coming out in March of 2015–**New to B2B: 90 Day Sales Rocket. An Outside Sales Hunter's Strategy to Blast Out Unbelievable Sales Numbers in 3 Months.** This book is for any outside sales person who wants to just knock the lights out of everybody else in the company. Be prepared to work hard because this strategy guarantees amazing results but it takes determination, discipline and at times an utter disregard for the time clock.

www.ingramcontent.com/pod-product-compliance
Lightning Source LLC
Chambersburg PA
CBHW070958180526
45168CB00003B/1196